Chocolate Therapy

DARE TO DISCOVER YOUR INNER CENTER!

MURRAY LANGHAM

Art concept and direction
Roger Simpson

TEN SPEED PRESS
Berkeley, California

Dedication

To chocolate lovers, the world over.

For my daughter Amelia Jayne
May she never lose sight of her guardian angel, who lights the path before her.

Acknowledgments

I thank all those who have allowed me to find my path in life: my mother Nancy, who loves chocolate, for childhood evenings around the TV with chocolates, chippies, and lemonade, and Roger Simpson for his therapeutic understanding of people and chocolate. I thank Robin Williamson, Ian Dempster, Renny and Raewyn Apprea (New Zealand), Mary Campbell-Cree (Australia), and David Goddard and Julia Christian (England), for their enthusiasm, encouragement, and support over more years than I care to remember. I am grateful to Anna Leslie and Peter Tait-Jamerson, for the debates and discussions from which this book has grown. And thanks to Andrew Stenson for his time and cyberspace knowledge; he has the patience of a saint. May you all walk in beauty and in peace.

Cover design by Catherine Jacobes
Interior design by Orca Publishing Services Ltd
Photography by Garth Des Forges

First published 1998 by Hazard Press, Christchurch, New Zealand

A Kirsty Melville Book

Ten Speed Press
P.O. Box 7123
Berkeley, California 94707
www.tenspeed.com

Distributed in Canada by Ten Speed Press Canada

Library of Congress Cataloging-in-Publication Data
Langham, Murray.
    Chocolate therapy : dare to discover your inner center! / Murray Langham.
       p.   cm.
    ISBN 1-58008-108-8 (pbk)
    1. Chocolate—Psychological aspects. 2. Chocolate—Therapeutic use. I. Title.
RZ999.L24 1999
615.8'9—dc21   99-22926
                                                     CIP

First printing, 1999
Printed in Hong Kong

1 2 3 4 5 6 7 8 9 10 — 03 02 01 00 99

contents

This book is about you and your relationship with chocolate—its shapes, its centers, its creamy, smooth milkiness, and its rich, dark bitterness. The following pages explore just what chocolate tells you about yourself and offer a guide for you to enjoy your life through chocolate. Read this guide from cover to cover, or open it at random and use it for daily inspiration.

How did this book come about? As a therapist I became curious about the great number of my clients who just *loved* chocolate. I began to observe what sort of chocolates and centers they liked, and I gained great insights into their behaviors. By incorporating this knowledge into my practice I've found that my clients move through issues and find their own centers faster than with most other therapeutic methods. Once people are centered they know where they're coming from, life begins anew, and magical transformations take place.

chocolate: a metaphor for life!

Chocolate: food from the gods

We each know what our favorite chocolate is. But what does that choice say about us? What does it mean when we eat the same type of chocolate, time and time again? Why do we crave that one flavor? Do we need to stop and take stock of our life—be it physical, emotional, mental, or spiritual?

There are, after all, many negative misconceptions about chocolate. Think of the signals we've been given by our parents, our teachers, our friends: "Chocolate is bad for you." "Only have one, no more." "You should be out finding a partner, not eating chocolate."

It's my belief that many of the "conditions" popularly attributed to chocolate are held in our bodies as guilt, and this stops us integrating with our real selves, prevents us from moving ahead, taking risks, living life to the full. Guilt disempowers us, stops us becoming who and what we want to be. Most of the chocolate beliefs that we have today are based on popular folklore, not on facts.

We have to stop living under this persecution. Chocolate is a fundamental part of our lives, so have fun with it and you'll find your life changes in ways you wouldn't believe. Chocolate is food from the gods; it's energy, vitality, oneness. Let's work with chocolate and add to our lives. Learn to grow and move through chocolate till you're in control once again.

Tasting chocolate

Chocolate is best on an empty stomach. I prefer it at room temperature, but the "official" view is that it's best at about 66°–77°F (19°–25°C).

Allow the chocolate to sit in your mouth for a few moments, to release its primary flavors and aromas. Then chew four to six times to mix the center with the sensuous chocolate. Allow that union to melt slowly in your mouth. Can't you taste it already? Then let it rest on the roof of your mouth, holding it with your tongue. Now close your eyes, if they aren't shut already, and enjoy your world of chocolate.

Chocolate Therapy

Chocolate Therapy is concerned with healing the body, mind, and spirit through liberation. Once self-realization around chocolate takes place, it allows you to restore, nourish, and rebalance the human psyche. When this happens, many other neuroses and fears just drop away.

Throughout history, researchers have acknowledged the profound influence of chocolate upon our physical, mental, emotional, and spiritual well-being. By focusing on one aspect of our lives and changing that, it resonates into all other areas of our existence, allowing us to integrate ourselves holistically.

Watch people when they choose a chocolate from a box. Or, better still, be conscious of how *you* go about it. Do you take forever to make that choice? Do you just grab one without looking? Do you read the selection card? Noticing even these things can cue you to look at your life and observe your innate decision-making strategies.

Do you take chocolates from the lower tray before the top tray is finished? This can indicate that you aren't happy with what life has placed before you. You could be looking for that hidden meaning to life. Chocolate Therapy helps you understand that if you don't find it within, you'll never find it, so it's important to take time out with chocolate and *find* your inner center.

Do you always take the same chocolate? Are you stuck in a rut, not willing to try something new? Meditating on chocolate can help you see how taking some risks will help you to move on in life.

And the chocolates that you don't like, what are they trying to tell you? Do they represent issues you don't want to face in your life? Maybe you really don't need the challenge. Only by finding your inner center will you uncover the real truth.

Do you eat chocolates alone? Do you save them? Do you hide them? Do you eat them as fast as you can? These are just some of the questions that can be answered through Chocolate Therapy.

How to use this book

There are several ways of using this book. The first is light-hearted fun with a box of chocolates and a group of friends at a dinner party.

1. Have everyone pick their favorite chocolate but resist the urge to eat until the box has gone around.
2. Once everyone has a chocolate and has noted the details of their choice—its shape, its center and the type of chocolate (milk, dark, bitter, white)—now you can eat and enjoy.
3. While doing so, one person reads from this book, starting with text about the *shape* each person has chosen. Or pass the book around and take turns to read out the text about your own choice.
4. Look at the pages about *centers*. Read out the text relating to the center chosen by each person.
5. See what the book says on pages 18–19 about the *type* of chocolate that each person has chosen.
6. Finally, check out what each person has done with the wrappers—their *post-chocolate behavior*.

You can also use this book for a more serious analysis. This may be on your own or with a group of friends. If there are more than five people, it's best to split into smaller groups and have a couple of copies of this book and a box of chocolates for each group.

1. Start by identifying an issue you'd like to resolve.
2. Pick out your favorite chocolate.
3. Look at its shape. What does it mean to you?
   (a) Look up the shape in the book and spend a couple of minutes looking at the photograph, taking note of responses you have to the shape in the photograph. This is a reflective time; what is it in the shape that you identify with?
   (b) Share your thoughts with the rest of the group.
   (c) Then read aloud what the book says about your shape, and share any feelings you have.
   (d) How does the shape fit in with your life?
4. What type of chocolate is it? (See pages 18–19.)
5. Take one bite and experience the flavor, the taste, the texture.

(a) Turn to the page featuring the center you've chosen and look at the photograph. How does it relate to you? Share this with the group.

(b) Read the words; other images may come to your mind. There is no right or wrong image, just *your* image. What are your intuitions, senses, thoughts, feelings? Look at the "excess": how do those qualities relate to you? Just take your time, and share and give feedback for others in the group.

6. Finish your chocolate and, as you do, bring the shape, the chocolate, and the center to your mind to integrate them as one. Spend a few more minutes reflecting on your life and your chocolate, and share any thoughts with the group.

7. Now look again at the issue you wanted to resolve. Are you any clearer? Discuss it with the group.

8. To finish, have a cup of coffee, tea, or hot chocolate and share the beautiful chocolates and enjoy them for being chocolate.

1

Have you considered what shape your favorite chocolate comes in? Is it round, oval, square? The shapes you're attracted to can indicate aspects of your personality and how you communicate.

When you're using Chocolate Therapy your choice should be based on instinct—select the shape you naturally drift towards. Your first impression is an unconscious response, which is usually the true one.

This part of this book explains in detail the shapes and what they mean to you. By looking at the images and meditating on these different shapes and symbols, you're likely to get glimpses of your true personality. These are the seven basic, archetypal shapes, with many layers and depths.

chocolate
shapes

As a circle person, you love company. In fact, you must be around people or life is not worth living. The original social butterfly, you love to party. You're likeable and friendly, attracting people because of your warmth. Your skill lies in working with people because you can read between the words and gestures. You have an empathy with others. In group situations you'll often ask, "Are you all happy with this?" "Are we seeing eye to eye?" You're a good listener, but you can lose sight of your own life in your quest for pleasing others.

You rarely put up a fight for what you believe in, as you don't like to upset others. You'll keep the peace at all costs. This means you can get trapped in other people's problems and find yourself going round and round in circles.

You like everything to be visually pleasing to yourself and others (the nice house, car, etc.), but this can sometimes make you deeply superficial.

In relationships you tend to flit from one person to another, trying to please, trying to shine. You tend to look only at the outer beauty. Once you start to see the inner beauty in others, and in yourself, you can really excel at relationships.

circle
I see

oval
I feel

As an oval person, you're moving beyond the circle, stretching your limits. You do this by using your feelings for others and, in turn, opening yourself to expressing your thoughts. You have a huge network of friends and contacts because you're socially adept and love making new friendships. You seem to know the right words for the right occasion, which can make you a good adviser. You work from the heart and go with what you feel, and are very creative within your own boundaries.

You're very good at promoting and creating enthusiasm for the ideas of others, if you believe in them. Your retentive memory and broad knowledge can sometimes shock your friends. As a feeling person, you may have been hurt in the past, which can mean you keep your own thoughts hidden. This can lead others to think that you're being manipulative and that they're being used.

You can inspire fear, because of your daredevil attitude, which can sometimes lead you to override other people's decisions.

You're very sensual and can spend time playing the field, but you'll then go on to have long, deep, and meaningful relationships. This is because you're allowing yourself to express your true feelings. You aren't afraid of experimenting in your love life.

As a square person, with all sides equal, you're balanced and therefore it's hard for others to push you around. This makes you honest and truthful. You love complying with authority. You base your judgments on facts and figures rather than intuition or guesswork; not too many surprises come your way.

You're very logical, analyzing problems systematically before reaching any conclusions. You follow directions meticulously and work in a structured way but, when making your own decisions, you can be unproductive, going over every little thing so that nothing gets done.

You have long-term friends who find you dependable, not prone to abrupt changes. Friends and colleagues feel safe to come to you for advice, although the rigidity of your approach can sometimes be frustrating.

You have an excellent memory. Sometimes you don't let others forget what should have being forgotten long ago.

You have an old-fashioned approach to partnership, romance, and love. You like to know your place. You form strong and lasting relationships. Your love life will be based on a sex manual to make sure you're doing it right.

square
I build

rectangle
I think

You're a very loyal person who loves sitting or staying in one place. You seem to be a rock for others to lean on. You calm those who are excited. Through your support, you allow people to feel needed.

As a rectangle, you have two sides the same as the square, which can mean stability, and two longer sides, which means you're moving out of the confines of the square and starting to express yourself and explore the hidden depths of your mind. You're known as a good listener, you offer friendship, and if you're asked to do anything for a friend, you'll do it as soon as you can. You enjoy organizing others and are good at doing for others what you find difficult to do for yourself.

You're excellent at concentrating and willing to broaden your horizons, so are happy to study for study's sake. This can make you the eternal student.

You have a fear of conflict and may help others to tolerate a situation rather than solve it. You do like to keep a low profile.

In relationships you like to express yourself through touch. You're a romantic, loving and very thoughtful towards your partner. You do need to make sure that your intention is matched by your actions. If there's any confrontation, your answer is to go to bed and enjoy.

spiral
Ignite

You're bursting with energy. Attracted to strange challenges, you love variety and like being involved in many activities. You're chaotic in your home life; your house can look as if a twister (a spiral!) has been through it. You can be an absolute whirlwind of activity.

You're abstracted and excitable; friends have to call your name many times before you answer. It's almost as if you're listening to the message of the universe and perhaps you are, because you're full of new ideas and very creative. You often change the subject, to the annoyance of your friends, and your communication can be disjointed because you're carrying so many ideas in your head.

No waiting with you; you don't like to stand in line. People tend to hold you back, which can save you from disaster. As an optimist, always looking to the future, you see things and say, "Why not? Let's try it." You get upset with people who are always looking at the negative without trying something first.

You're just as chaotic in your love life, but you enjoy relationships to the full. You like to make the first move in romance. Sometimes you'll find it fun just to slow down and let others take the lead, but not as often as you should. You can run hot and cold about sex, but when you're hot, you're hot.

triangle
I can

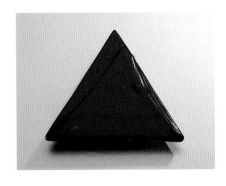

As a triangular person, you're a mover and a shaker. You don't have time to read this because you're out there making things happen.

You like getting immediate results and enjoy solving problems, making quick decisions. You have the gift of the gab and can talk your way out of most situations. That's just as well because, as a triangle person with three sharp points, you can push yourself into some strange situations. You like to be the leader and make your own rules. You'll accept all acknowledgments of your achievements, but any failures you're likely to blame on others.

As a high achiever, you love to succeed because you're positive and never let go. Paperwork and the humdrum details of life bore you. You seldom worry about other people's feelings and therefore can override or bulldoze others.

You can find that you change your jobs and towns or houses often because you thrive on challenge. You've no time for people who don't keep up with you.

Your relationships tend to be a little one-sided. You're not too concerned with your partner as long as you're having a good time. If things get a little deep, it's time to move on. Partners stay with you because life is never boring.

As a diamond person you have an innocence about you, as if you have all eternity to play with. After all, diamonds are forever! You make decisions slowly, after internalizing them, and only move on to a new project or relationship when you feel from deep within you that this is right. You may even meditate or spend time in contemplation. You love children, pets, and the little things in life.

Most areas of your life are filled with a deep conviction that what you're doing is right for the planet and the people on it. You share with others any praise or credit when you succeed. If you fail, you'll take the blame. You prefer to do something yourself rather than ask others, because they may not do it as well as you.

You're a person who enjoys life and what money can buy—you like expensive objects—but you're not flamboyant.

You find yourself surrounded by people who have integrity. You have no time for the superficial.

You like to be made love to in nice surroundings—champagne in a lovely restaurant, with all the trimmings—and are at your best in these places. To you, love and sex aren't to be taken lightly. You're deeply committed to your partner and would never even consider having an affair.

diamond

I am

Types of chocolate

The different types of chocolate are made with varying percentages of cocoa butter, cocoa solids, and sugar; in most cases, vanilla is added. The chocolate beans are a mixture from around the world, depending on what flavor is required. A good chocolate will snap when broken. If it splinters, it's too dry; if it bends and is hard to break, it's too waxy. Chocolate must be shiny in appearance, smooth to hold, and start to melt in the hand. It should smell like chocolate, not like the sugar it contains. Chocolate appeals to all our senses: hearing, sight, touch, smell, and taste. This completeness, this balance, is why we adore chocolate.

White

You have all the power of the universe behind you if only you knew what you wanted in life. All options are open to you, but which one to take? It can be hard to make decisions because of all the choices you have. Always weighing up the pros and cons, you can see both sides of an argument. This can cloud your thoughts, but when you make a decision you have all the force with you.

Milk

As a lover of milk chocolate, you like to live in the past emotionally, to love that sweet, smooth feeling that is the pure essence of childhood. You're remembering past happiness, a time when things were simple and straightforward.

Dark

You're a forward-looking person. Your thoughts are always directed towards the future—"How can I do this differently?" You have a fertile and active mind that is always refining. Although, for you, the past is the past, this doesn't stop you from collecting *objets d'art*. This can mean you like material possessions.

Bitter

A connoisseur of the fine things in life, you know what you're talking about and you're a specialist in your field. This can make you dictatorial in your dealings with others. People have to fit into your idea of living, otherwise you'll have no time for them.

All chocolate

If you're a person who loves all types of chocolate, your loyalties lie with chocolate itself. So you're a person who is flexible and can fit into any situation anytime, anywhere. You have an all-around knowledge of all walks of life. You can move with the times and keep up with the information age. You don't like to be left behind.

2

When we choose a center, a filling that we like (indeed, love!)—whether it be in a box of chocolates or our favorite chocolate bar —what is it that attracts us? Is it the smell, the texture on our tongue and teeth, the color, the taste?

These centers link into our own subconscious mind or the inner part that guides our emotions, our moods, our inner thoughts, our self-esteem. By understanding the meanings of the centers, we can begin to see what is guiding us through the complexities of life.

chocolate centers

almond

Climbing the almond tree of prosperity, you desire success and you like to celebrate your achievements. You have a quickness of mind that can stagger your friends. You can change your conversation or your beliefs very rapidly. You love making changes to yourself and others. You may even argue with yourself, because there are so many thoughts in your head. You like to offer a hand in friendship and are keen to help others.

Excess You can appear flippant to people who do not know you. You have the best of intentions, but some people just don't want to be changed, so stop trying. You may rely on helping hands from others when you could do something yourself.

apricot

You're a gentle and patient person, very self-assured, certain of who and what you are. You're able to access the wisdom of the past and bring it, with love, to others. You can serve humanity by helping others, whether you're an office or factory worker, a caregiver, or are operating at the spiritual level. You do like to have boundaries and live in warm, cozy surroundings.

Excess A sign of unrequited love. A shortage of patience and believing that only you can do something well enough. Lacking in self-esteem, not believing in yourself. Looking at the material world as if that's all there is. The need to be comforted, but not trusting others.

brazilnut

As a person who loves brazilnuts, you're very diplomatic and cultured. You love style and elegance; your clothes are always the latest fashion. You like everything to look right and you have a place for everything. You read the latest book and see the latest play. You like to be seen at all the right places with the right faces. But is the carnival of life an act, or is it real?

Excess   Being so busy with the physical and material that you get buried in it and end up laughing on the outside, crying on the inside. Keeping people at arm's length. Where is your life? Where's your love for yourself? What mask are you wearing today?

caramel–soft

Without making a fuss, you conscientiously get things done. You're dependable and steady, and friends can rely on you. They call you an angel. You have an aptitude for figures, and you enjoy playing with money. You can bargain as well as any horse trader. Friends talk to you or invite you along when any large purchases are in the offing. You don't miss much—you have an eye like an eagle.

Excess   Feeling lost and confused if you move away from your set routine. Finding it difficult to be flexible or to bend to other people's point of view. Money to you is your security.

caramel–hard

You have all the attributes of soft caramel but you crystallize that softness to give you a solid base. You're firm in your dealings with others and very law-abiding. Your integrity is never questioned. You're never late; you always clean up after yourself. You're a rock for others to lean on. You live to work; anything that you do will be achieved by hard labor, which satisfies you. You can be security conscious.

Excess Getting lost in life's trivia. Having fixed ideas about most things and preaching these to others but not listening to what others are saying. It could be time to remove your crown and join in.

cherry

You're full of energy, creating around yourself a virtual whirlwind of excitement. You love sex, passion, lust and life, the ups and downs of relationships. Watching your lifestyle can make your friends tired. When you feel passionate about a cause, you can drive everyone else mad. For you, life's a bowl of cherries—only you'd like them all at once.

Excess   Lacking in energy, feeling lethargic. Living through relationships—the current relationship is far more exciting than the last one, or far better than anyone else's. Possibility of anger and flare-ups.

chocolate

As a chocolate lover, you're part of the advancement of the human race, looking to the future. You're a proactive person who respects other people's points of view. You realize that there's more to life than what you see. You can find yourself relaxed and enjoying the game of life, which you join in willingly. You can laugh at yourself and don't take yourself too seriously.

No chocolate   You're in denial and perhaps need to see a chocolate therapist. There's no substitute for chocolate, so stop trying to find one. Start living.

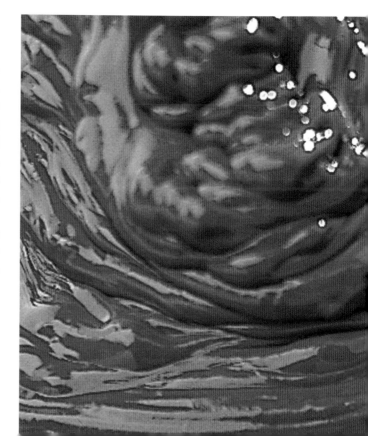

coconut

You dream of island hideaways in sun, sand, and surf. You're a lotus-eater who needs to be near water, which is very important to you. You're a passionate person, and this can allow you to be creative and artistic. You love to meditate through music and the movement of dance. You find yourself drawn to the beat of drums, the energy of the earth beat, the rhythm of life.

Excess   Burying your head in the sand, not facing reality, not connecting with earth's energies. Haziness of mind can be an issue.

coffee

As a coffee person, you're not one to be kept waiting or standing in line. You like everything at once, and why not? You're a deep thinker and like the buzz of discussion and debate. After all, this is why coffee and chocolate houses came into being. Your mind is like a parachute—it works best when open.

Excess Living on a caffeine fix, nervous energy, prone to addictions. You can be impatient and throw tantrums when things don't go your way. You always look busy, but what are you achieving?

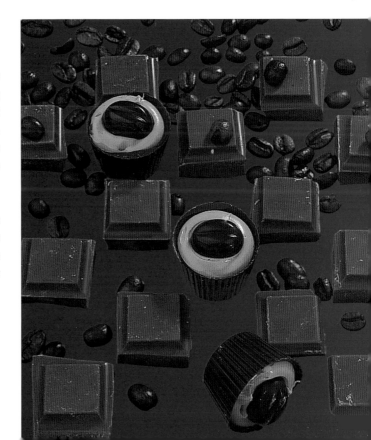

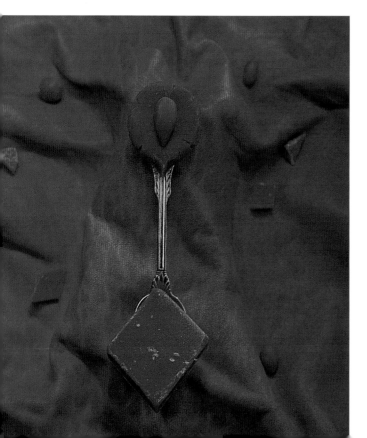

fudge

As a lover of fudge you're sensual and smooth, gliding through life as if you were born with a silver spoon in your mouth. You don't seek to be above others; it's just that you're a little different and special, seeking to be the best you can. You do like to shop, or is it retail therapy? Your thoughts are very expansive, but you're not sure why. You're always looking at your role in the big picture.

Excess   The frustration of not being able to achieve what you want. Getting yourself into sticky situations, time and time again.

ginger

You're one of the world's achievers. You have energy, drive, ambition, and vision; what you can imagine, you can obtain. Many ginger lovers have success and power, and they've worked for it. In the past, ginger was a very masculine energy, but now the feminine energy is combining with that to allow you to work smarter, not harder.

Excess   As a dreamer, loving to sit back and let others do the planning. Your planning is in your mind, a fantasy of love, success, and power, in which money also plays an important role. You very seldom tell anyone these thoughts, because you're a very private person.

hazelnut

You're a person who works with the wisdom of mother earth. You're aware of the energies around you and are in harmony with nature. This gives you an inner knowing, and you may find that you're in the right place at the right time. Fertility, of the body or of the mind, is often associated with this center. Some people may see you as lucky, but you understand that you're just a vehicle for the knowledge flowing through you.

Excess   Trying too hard to be a "greenie." Finding yourself wanting to be invisible. Being shy and staying in the background.

honeycomb crunch

You're a person who isn't afraid to try something new. You have plenty of ideas and you can turn these into gold. Although some of your concepts could be built on crumbling foundations, that doesn't stop you or hold you back. You just move on to the next project. You're a person who enjoys life; for you, the journey is more important than the destination. Could you be chasing the rainbow?

Excess You're looking for refinement in life, with a few rough edges to chisel down. You remember your parents' phrases—"You can do better"; "You're not as clever as your sister/brother." A chip off the old block.

lemon

This love of lemon can mean that you're an old soul, someone who has been here many times. You're very much your own boss. Not worried about what other people think of you, you do your own thing. You have a sharp wit and win most debates. You enjoy exploring your mind or others, all the time learning new concepts and ideas. You're a keen player in the information age.

Excess   Where's the joy in your life? You can be nervous, anxious, tending to put yourself down, not speaking out or standing up to others, being just a doormat.

lime

You know where you're going; you're very direct, straight to the point. You have a good sense of direction in your life. You listen to your heart and can speak of your feelings and often act on them. You must have space and will go to extraordinary lengths to be able to sit in a garden or a park, or by a lake or river, whenever you feel hemmed in or claustrophobic.

Excess   Decision making takes a long time. You have no direction and can be all over the place. You may have suffered in the past, so you've closed down, too afraid to expose your heart to love again.

marshmallow

As a person who likes marshmallow, you're very social. You like to party, to have people around you. Light and fluffy, you can move from one idea or subject to the next, without a great deal of thought. If you choose pink marshmallow, you're in love with romance and very optimistic. White marshmallow denotes clarity for that moment in time.

Excess   You can get bored very quickly. Tend to agree with whomever you are talking to at the time, no matter what you believe in. Not a lot of follow-through on ideas that you come up with. The need for romance, for clarity.

orange

You're excellent in emergency situations. A caregiver of the highest order, you can feel a deep sense of need to help people who are in shock or who are sick. You can follow commands easily. You need to aspire to higher things in your life, to discover yourself through a teacher or a guru, to fulfill your spiritual needs. In you, energy and wisdom move together for the betterment of humanity.

Excess Codependency to a teacher. Only dealing with the here and now, no time for anything else. This can mean there has been shock and trauma in the past and you haven't dealt with it.

peanut

You love outdoor activities, sports, and team games, whether you're playing or watching in person or on television. You're the salt of the earth, the mainstream of society. You're happy with where you are in life, just getting on with it and doing the best you can for yourself and your family. You have strong views on matters that concern your loved ones and their environment. Time is precious to you, and you fit a lot into your day.

Excess   Living in your own little world and getting caught up in small-town mentality. Overdoing involvement in a neighborhood, a sports club, or a church group at the expense of your own family. You're always running out of time.

pecan

Pecan lovers are searching for eternal youth, the elixir of life, the stone of the wise. You like to show that you're connected to earthly things and family traditions. You may appear at times to be ponderous in your thoughts because you feel a need to be right and say the right things.

Excess You could miss the real issues of living by being caught up in the struggle to stay young; vanity could be an issue here. You're a visual person who can really sparkle when your face reflects your inner youth and wisdom.

peppermint

All things are possible to peppermint lovers; you have all the scope of life to choose from. You tend to see life as moving on—tomorrow is another day. You're very clear on what you're doing, whether it be in matters of the heart or in your profession. You're full of ideas and won't be bound by rules unless you've made them. You're always striving for things to be better, looking ahead with an open mind.

Excess   The need for all the above. Being able to let go and trust your inner center. Suffering from the past is clouding your judgment of the here and now.

pineapple

Facing the world with joy and happiness, you can see the hidden potential in everyone you meet. Because you have a strong mind that thrives on challenges, you can achieve many and varied things in this life, with a sense of fun and adventure. You like being in learning situations, going back to university, or attending college. You also enjoy interacting with people of like mind. You have a strong relationship with the sun; in fact, you could be a sun worshipper from the past

Excess You could suffer from SAD (seasonal affective disorder)—you need the sun. Can be living on your nerves and may even develop an acid tongue.

raspberry

You seek the innocence of a child, the fun times of the past when it seemed as if there was only black or white and life was so simple. As a lover of raspberry, you find yourself labeling and gathering people and things almost as if they could be put into pigeonholes. You have a great sense of protection and loyalty to your nearest and dearest. You're a person who starts and loves collections.

Excess   The need to be protected. You don't throw anything away, as you never know when it will come in handy. Because you love to collect things, people could see you as a hoarder. Without a name for people and objects you feel lost, naive, and out of step with what's happening around you.

strawberry

You're a loving and caring person. In touch with your intuition, you listen to other people's problems with compassion and tenderness. You have or will find time for people and you believe that things will turn out all right in the end. A romantic and an idealist at heart, you have lots of unconditional love for yourself and for others. Music can play a large part in your life.

Excess Disappointments in love not being returned. Sensitivity to others can leave you drained of energy. The need to love at any cost means you can be living through others, seeing the world through rose-colored glasses.

turkish delight

You're a person on a spiritual quest. The material life doesn't satisfy you; you know that there must be more to life. You seek to open your heart to the influence of the cosmos so that the love of the Great Spirit of the universe can flow through you. You're a very forthright and honest person. You can meditate, sitting still for hours and allowing your mind to be creative and in tune, so that you feel balanced and complete.

Excess Looking for a guru or needing to be in groups to feel part of a spiritual society. You can get lost in others' ideas and depend too much on spiritual teachers, not thinking your own thoughts. Trying to escape from reality.

walnut

You have a solid heart of gold. You love the outdoors—the forests, the parks, the mountains. You have a fresh approach to problem solving and to living. You communicate well, whether it be in person or in writing, and this could mean you like the arts. Poems, plays, and novels are all part of your expression of your subconscious, which others may see as profound. For you, it's assisting people to remember what they already know.

Excess   A thin veneer of refinement. Because you can be a solitary person, happy in your own space, people find you hard to get to know. A lack of expression can lead to depression. The need to look at how you communicate to yourself and to others.

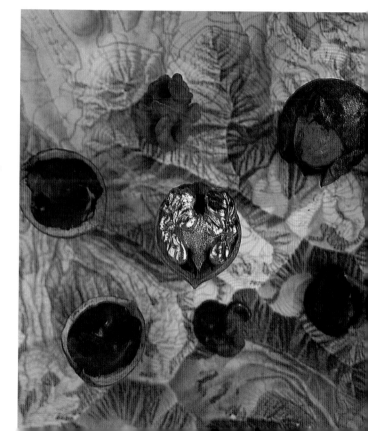

3

Your attitudes to sex can be linked to how you handle the paper or foil that surrounds your chocolate. Look, too, at what you (or, better still, your friends) do with bus, theater, and movie tickets!

*post-chocolate
behavior*

the scruncher

Do you just scrunch the paper up and throw it away without a second glance? This can mean that you're missing many signals to do with love and sex. You can be missing the subtleties of the look, the touch, the sounds of someone wooing you. You have lots of scattered thoughts and it can be difficult for you to concentrate on one subject at a time. Even in bed your mind wanders. You enjoy sex for what it is but you really don't know what all the fuss is about.

the folder

Do you fold the paper flat, as if you had all the time in the world? This can mean that your bedroom is always tidy, your drawers and cupboards neat and clean. You have thoughts that are orderly and methodical. For you, making love comes after wining and dining and all the right moves. You may even have a few sex manuals, as it has to be done right and, of course, only in a bed—your bed. Bathing after making love isn't an option for you; it's a necessity.

the baller

Do you shape the paper into a ball and play with it on the table? You may be bored with your sex life; you need some excitement. Perhaps it's time to move out of your comfort zone, to expand the horizons of your love life. You can be jealous and this can hold you back from really exploring your sex and sexuality. You have sex wherever you can, but the fulfillment may be missing.

the tearer

Do you tear the paper into long strips, to see how long you can get them? This can indicate a challenge when it comes to sex. Was this better than the last time or your last lover? You need approval and are always trying to prove yourself, apparently to others but actually to yourself. You have difficulty in holding on to personal relationships, because you believe you may be missing something by staying with one partner.

the sculptor

Do you like to fashion birds, chalices, trees, and so on from your chocolate wrapper? This means you need an outlet for your creative potential. In bed you can be dynamite, very imaginative with sex. You could be involved in tantric practices to further enhance the charm and charisma of your lovemaking. You're a nature lover, so outdoor sex is fine by you. Anyone you're with will feel special, because you love to touch and play.

the smoother

Do you smooth the paper with your fingernail or a coin until it is absolutely flat? This can mean that you love to massage, to stroke your partner, for hours at a time. You're a very sensual person, using your fingernails to send shivers down your partner's spine. You also like—need—to be touched; otherwise your creativity and inspiration tend to dry up. For you, foreplay is just as important as, if not more important than, sex itself.

the roller

Do you make your paper into a tube? This can mean that you like to play Cupid, blowing imaginary darts through your little cylinder. A matchmaker at heart, you like to meddle in other people's love life, but what about your own? The grass always looks greener on the other side, but does your side need some water? Does this mean you are hollow and vacuous, or does it mean you'd like other people to experience the happiness that you've found?

the twister

If you twist the paper into a stick or tight rope, this indicates that you live on your nerves. You can be jumpy and may need a good relaxing massage to unwind. (How much you need this can be shown by how tightly you've twisted your wrapper.) When making love, you don't allow yourself to let go and move with the flow. To forget your performance nerves, just be yourself.

no wrappers

If you like your chocolate without the mystery of a wrapper, you don't like surprises when it comes to lovemaking; what you see is what you get. It's all or nothing for you, no in-betweens. You know what you like and you go for it. You're not fooled by appearances. You can see beneath the wrappings, the glitter, and the glamour. You can be a little impatient in bed, sometimes forgetting foreplay. You get a great deal of satisfaction from sex.

MURRAY LANGHAM, therapist, counselor, and facilitator, first became aware of the possibilities of chocolate through his early work as a chef and restaurant owner. As his interest in people developed, he studied and gained diplomas in clinical hypnotherapy and neuro-linguistic programming. Using these modalities Murray has evolved a new way of understanding the self through chocolate as a means for change. He wrote this book in the wild landscape of the lower North Island of New Zealand.

For more information about Chocolate Therapy and details of seminars, please contact:

> CHOICE SEMINARS
> P.O. BOX 2453
> WELLINGTON
> NEW ZEALAND

E-mail: choiceseminars@clear.net.nz

ROGER SIMPSON, New Zealand-born artist and therapist, pioneered therapeutic horticultural and intensive Art/Earth therapy programs. He continues broad-spectrum therapies and has extended the psychology of the creative spark to the photographs and images in this book.